MACHINES

CONTENTS

WHAT IS A MACHINE?

Thousands of different devices are machines, from calculators to trucks. Many do not really look like something you might think of as a machine. Some, such as scissors and staplers, are very simple machines. Others, such as computers and cars, are very complicated. All machines, however, have one thing in common – they help us do jobs and so make our lives easier. Try thinking about what you did yesterday and write down every machine you used or saw, from when you woke up to when you went back to bed. We are surrounded by machines, wherever we are and whatever we are doing. They provide us with vital help – many things we take for granted, such as opening a tin can or tightening a screw, can only be done with a machine. This book looks at some of the most familiar machines, from the very simplest to some of the most complex.

Screwdriver

Pliers

Scissors

Hammer

Allen keys

All these tools are simple machines that you might have at home. They each do a job that would be much more difficult without them.

Using tools

This girl is using a spanner to do up the nuts on her model. A spanner is a simple tool that is used to tighten up, or undo, nuts. Using the spanner is much better than using her fingers alone, because she can make joints much tighter and more secure.

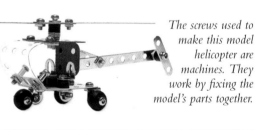

The screws used to make this model helicopter are machines. They work by fixing the model's parts together.

FACT BOX

• Leonardo da Vinci (1452–1519) was an Italian artist and inventor. He drew plans for machines, such as tanks and aircraft, that were centuries ahead of their time.

• Greek scientist Hero of Alexandria lived in the 1st century AD. He invented a steam engine, a slot machine and a screw press.

Old machines

This picture was painted in about 1400. It shows people using many different machines to help them farm the land. Some of the first machines ever invented were used by farmers. At the bottom of the picture is a plough and on the right-hand side is a water-wheel. At the very top is a machine called a shaduf, which was used to raise water from a deep well.

You can see huge machines, such as diggers and cranes, on construction sites. The machines have powerful engines for moving and lifting soil, rocks, steel and concrete.

This woman is using a hand axe to chop large logs into smaller pieces. When she brings the axe down, the sharp blade slices into the wood, forcing it to split apart. The axe is a simple machine, but it is very effective.

Unlike the other machines shown here, a computer does not help you lift, move or cut things. Instead it helps make your life easier by remembering information and doing calculations for you. Computers help us to work much faster and more accurately.

THE FIRST MACHINES

ALL machinery is based on the elements found in six simple machines. These six machines are: the lever, the wheel and axle, the inclined plane or ramp, the wedge, the screw and the pulley. All these machines have been used for thousands of years, but the simplest and probably the oldest is the lever. Any rod or stick can act as a lever, helping you to move heavy objects or prise things apart. A lever is a bar or rod that tilts on a pivot. A small effort pushing down on the longer end can raise a large weight on the shorter end nearer the pivot. When it is used like this, the lever makes the power of your push into a much larger push. This is called a mechanical advantage. There are several different types of lever. Some have just one lever arm, while others have two lever arms joined together by a pivot.

A door is a simple lever. Its pivot is made by the hinges. Closing a door at the handle is much easier than pressing near the hinge.

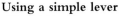

Using a simple lever
This girl is using a spoon as a simple lever to lift the lid off a tin of paint. The lever arm pivots on the lip of the tin. As the girl pushes down on the long end, the shorter end wedged under the lid lifts it up with great force, making the stiff lid move.

Effort

Pivot

Load

How a lever works
A push or a pull is the force put on one part of the lever arm. This is called the effort. The force you are trying to overcome is the weight of the object. This is called the load.

Levers and lifting

This boy is using a ruler as a lever to lift a book. With the pivot (the small box) near the book, only a small effort is needed to lift the book up. The lever makes the boy's push larger.

When the pivot is moved so that it is in the middle of the lever, the effort needed to lift the book up is equal to the book's weight. The effort and the load are the same.

When the pivot is near where the boy is pressing, more effort is needed to lift the book. The force of the push needed to lift the book is now larger than the weight of the book.

This lever machine is a shaduf. It is being used to water fields. A long pole on a frame has a bucket on one end and heavy logs tied to the other. The effort needed to raise the water is not made by the boy, but by the heavy weight.

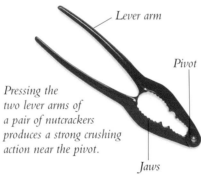

Lever arm

Pivot

Pressing the two lever arms of a pair of nutcrackers produces a strong crushing action near the pivot.

Jaws

A pair of levers

A pair of nutcrackers, like a pair of scissors or a pair of pliers, has two lever arms joined at a pivot. Pressing the ends of the nutcracker arms together squashes the nut in its jaws. The levers make the effort you use about four times bigger, allowing you to break the nut quite easily.

LEVERS AND BALANCE

Levers are not just used for lifting, cutting and squashing. A lever on a central pivot can be made to balance. The lever will balance if the effect of the forces on one side of the pivot is the same as the effect of the forces on the other. A playground see-saw is a balancing lever. It is a plank balanced on a centre post or pivot. Using a see-saw, someone small and light can balance a much bigger person if they sit in the right position. Outside the playground, balancing levers have important uses. By using a lever to balance one force with another, the size of one force can be compared to the size of another. This is how a weighing machine called a balance scale works. It measures the mass (weight) of an object by comparing it with standard masses such as grams and kilograms.

This is the sort of balance scale once used for weighing things in shops or in the kitchen. To make the lever arm balance, the weights on the left must equal the weight in the pan.

Using a balance scale
To weigh an object in a balance, the object is put in a pan resting on one end of the lever arm. Weights are added to the other end of the arm until it balances. Then the individual weights are added up to find the object's weight.

A Roman lever balance
This carving, from the 1st century AD, shows a Roman balance. The object to be weighed was put in the sack and a large weight was moved backwards and forwards until the arm balanced.

Two children of equal weight, the same distance from the pivot, make the see-saw balance.

Lever arm   Pivot

Balancing a see-saw

A see-saw shows the effect of moving a weight nearer or farther from the pivot of a lever arm. Two children of equal weight, the same distance from the pivot, make a see-saw balance. But if another child is added to one end, the arm overbalances to that side. By moving the single child farther from the pivot, or the pair closer to it, the arm balances again.

By adding another child to one side, that side overbalances. The pair's greater weight easily lifts the lighter boy.

FACT BOX

• A trebuchet was a medieval war machine based on the lever arm. It was used to hurl boulders at the enemy up to 0.5 km away.

• Balance scales were invented by the ancient Egyptians so that they could weigh out gold. Gold was a precious commodity, so it needed to be weighed accurately.

By moving the pair nearer the pivot, their weight can be balanced by the lighter boy moving farther away.

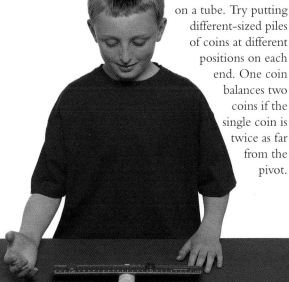

Investigating balance

Make a ruler balance on a tube. Try putting different-sized piles of coins at different positions on each end. One coin balances two coins if the single coin is twice as far from the pivot.

LEVERS EVERYWHERE

L EVERS are very common machines. On these pages you can see some of the machines that use levers to work. Each one has a diagram to show you where the pivot, effort and load, are to help you see how the lever is working. Lever machines are divided into three different classes, or basic kinds, of lever. The most common type is a first-class lever, where the pivot is always between the load and the effort. Balances and pliers are types of first-class lever. In a second-class lever the load is between the pivot and the effort. Nutcrackers and wheelbarrows are two examples of second-class levers. Finally, in a third-class lever the effort is between the pivot and the load. Hammers and tweezers are third-class levers.

Every key on a piano keyboard is a lever and has several other levers attached to it. The levers make a hammer fly quickly against a string when the key is pressed.

In a pair of pliers, the effort is pressing down on handles. The load is the resistance of an object in the jaws of the pliers.

Lifting the handles of a wheelbarrow lifts a heavy load nearer the pivot, or wheel.

First-class levers
A pair of pliers has two lever arms linked at the pivot by a hinge. They are first-class levers because the handles are on one side of the pivot and the jaws are on the other.

Second-class levers
A wheelbarrow does not look like a lever, but it is one. The lever arm goes from the end of the handle to the centre of the wheel, which is the pivot. A small effort pulling up on the handles lifts the load in the barrow.

A hammer acts as a lever when you use your wrist as a pivot. Your fingers make the effort to lift the hammer's head.

Pivot Effort

Load

Third-class levers

A hammer may not look like a lever, but it is. The handle joins with your hand to make the lever arm, with your wrist making the pivot. Your fingers supply the effort to make the hammer head move down.

A fishing rod is a third-class lever. When it lifts a fish out of the water, a pull much larger than the weight of the fish is needed. But to cast out the line, a small movement of the fisherman's arm makes a big movement at the end of the rod. This flicks the end of the line a long way.

Your arm makes a third-class lever. As it lifts up an object, the effort is between the pivot and the load.

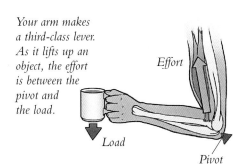

Effort

Load

Pivot

Body levers

The lower bones in your arm form a third-class lever with the pivot at your elbow. The muscle at the front of your upper arm is called the biceps. It makes the effort to lift up a weight in your hand, which is the load.

MAKING LEVERS WORK

You will need: short pencil, two pieces of wood each about 15 cm long, thick elastic bands, objects to pick up or squash such as sweets or grapes.

O N these pages you can find out how to make two different lever machines. The first is a simple gripper for picking up or squashing objects. It can act both as a pair of nutcrackers, which is a second-class lever, or a pair of tweezers, which is a third-class lever. The class, or type, of lever it is changes according to where the effort and load are. In a pair of nutcrackers, the load (in this case a sweet) is between the pivot (the pencil) and the effort (where you push). In a pair of tweezers, the effort is between the pivot and the load. Draw a lever diagram for both ways to use the machine to help you understand how each one works.

The second machine is a balance scale. It is like the ones used by the Romans about 2,000 years ago. It works by balancing the weight of an object against a known weight, in this case a bag of coins. The coins are moved along the lever arm until they balance the object being weighed. The object's weight is then read off against a scale.

Make a gripper

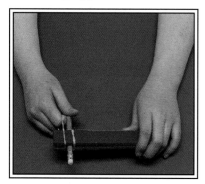

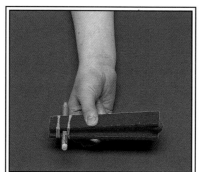

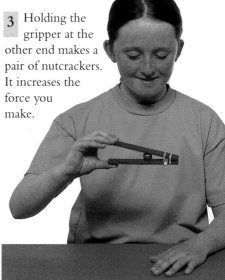

3 Holding the gripper at the other end makes a pair of nutcrackers. It increases the force you make.

1 Put the pencil between the two pieces of wood, near one end. Wrap the elastic bands tightly around the pieces of wood to make a pivot. You have now made the gripper.

2 Hold the gripper near the pivot to make it act like a pair of tweezers. See if you can pick up a delicate object, such as a sweet or a grape, without crushing the object.

Make a balance scale

You will need: thick card about 50 cm x 8 cm, thin card, scissors, string, ruler, hole punch, 12 cm circle of card, sticky tape, 100 g of coins, felt tip pen, objects to weigh.

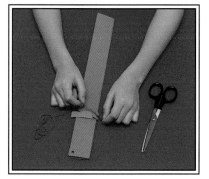

1 Make the arm by folding the thick card in two. Make a loop of thin card and attach it to the arm so that its centre is 11 cm from one end. Tie a piece of string to this support.

2 Make a hole 1 cm from the arm's end. Make the card circle into a cone-shaped pan and tie it to the hole. Make an envelope and tie it to a loop so that it hangs over the arm.

3 Put the 100 g of coins in the envelope and seal it up. Starting from the centre of the support, make a mark every 5 cm along the arm. This scale will tell you the weight of an object.

4 To weigh an object, put it in the pan and slide the envelope of coins backwards and forwards along the arm until the arm balances. Each mark along the scale equals 50 g. So, in this picture, the object being weighed is about 75 g.

WHEELS AND AXLES

Pushing on the pedals of this child's tricycle turns the axle and drives the tricycle's front wheel.

THE wheel is one of the most important inventions ever made. About 6,000 years ago, people discovered that using logs as rollers was a more efficient way of moving heavy loads. A slice from a log was the first wheel and connecting a pole to a wheel made an axle.

A wheel on the end of an axle makes a simple machine. Turning the wheel makes the axle turn, too. This might not seem like a machine, but it is because turning the axle is easier using the wheel than turning the axle on its own. Wheels and axles increase mechanical advantage – turning the wheel makes the axle turn with greater force. The bigger the wheel compared to the size of the axle, the greater the force, making turning even easier. Wheels are used in millions of machines. One of the most obvious is in wheeled vehicles, which were in use more than 4,000 years ago and are still the most common form of transport today. Sometimes wheel and axle machines are difficult to recognize. Can you find a wheel and axle in a spanner or a door key?

— Handle

— Spindle

Winding up

The key of a wind-up toy has a handle that is a wheel and a spindle that is an axle. The large handle makes it easier to turn the spindle. Door keys work in the same way.

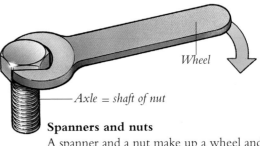

Wheel

Axle = shaft of nut

Spanners and nuts

A spanner and a nut make up a wheel and axle system. The threaded shaft of the nut is the axle and the handle of the spanner is the wheel. By turning the spanner, it is much easier to tighten or loosen the nut.

Cart wheels

This Roman mosaic picture was made about 1,700 years ago. It shows a cart full of wine grapes being pulled by oxen. The wheels and axles on a cart like this meant that the oxen could pull a much heavier load than they could carry. The first cart wheels were made from slices of tree trunk. Spokes were invented about 4,000 years ago.

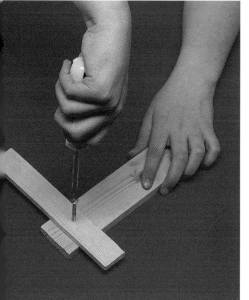

A screwdriver's shaft is an axle and its handle a wheel. The handle increases the force on the shaft when it is turned to drive in a screw.

Potter's wheels

One of the first uses of the wheel was to make pots. Simple potter's wheels, such as this one in India, are still used around the world. The massive wooden wheel is turned by foot or by hand.

Steering wheels

A car's steering wheel is attached to the end of an axle, called the steering column. The wheel increases the force from the driver's hands, so giving the driver enough force to control the car.

WHEELS AT WORK

THERE are hundreds of different examples of wheels and axles. Some are very old designs, such as the capstan wheel. A capstan is a wheel on an axle with handles that stretch out from the edge of the wheel. The handles are used to turn the wheel, which turns the axle. Large capstan wheels can be turned by animals as they walk round and round, or by several people who each push on a handle. In the past, they were a familiar sight on ships and in dockyards where they were used to raise heavy loads such as a ship's anchor. This project shows you how to make a simple capstan wheel for lifting a weight that works in a similar way. At the end of the project a ratchet is attached to the axle. A ratchet is a very useful device that acts like a catch. It prevents the capstan wheel turning back on itself once you have stopped winding it.

This water-raising machine has a capstan wheel. To operate the machine, a person or animal pushes on the handle and walks round and round. This raises a gate, allowing water from the canal to flow into the fields.

Make a capstan wheel

1 Draw a line about one-third from the top of the box on each side. Use this as a guide to draw around the tube to make circles on opposite sides of the box. Cut out the circles.

2 Cut four slots in one end of the tube. Lay two pieces of dowelling into the slots so that they cross over. Tape the dowelling in place. You have now made the capstan wheel.

3 Push the tube into the holes in the box. Tape the end of a piece of string to the middle of the tube inside the box. Tie a heavy object to the other end of the string.

4 Stand the box on a table edge so the weight hangs down. Turn the capstan wheel to lift the object. Try turning the handles at their ends and then near the centre of the wheel.

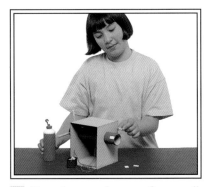

5 To make a ratchet, cut four small pieces of card and carefully glue them to the tube at the opposite end to the capstan wheel. These will form the ratchet teeth.

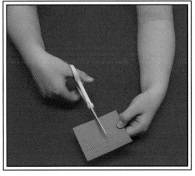

6 From a piece of thick card, cut an L-shaped piece. Bend one of the legs of the L at a right angle to the other leg. This will form the part that locks into the ratchet teeth.

MATERIALS

You will need: pencil, small cardboard box such as a shoe box, ruler, card tube, scissors, dowelling, sticky tape, string, a weight, thick card, glue.

7 Glue the L card to the top of your box so that the end hanging over the edge just catches in the ratchet teeth. Leave the glue to dry before trying your ratchet.

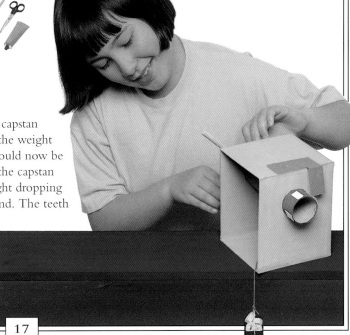

8 Wind up the capstan wheel to lift the weight up again. You should now be able to let go of the capstan without the weight dropping back to the ground. The teeth will catch on the L shape, stopping the axle from turning backwards.

INCLINED PLANES

How can an inclined plane, or ramp, be a machine? It is a type of machine because it makes going uphill, or moving an object uphill against the force of gravity, much easier. Think about a removal van and people trying to lift a heavy box inside it. It might take two people working together to lift the box up high enough to reach into the van. But one person could push the box up a gently sloping ramp on his or her own. You often see planks used as ramps on a building site. Also, walking uphill on a winding path is using a ramp. It is much easier to walk up a gently sloping path that twists and turns than it is to climb straight up a very steep hillside. You have to walk farther along the gentle slope to reach the top of the hill, but it is much easier.

These are the remains of a huge mud-brick ramp used by the ancient Egyptians to build a temple at Karnac about 3,000 years ago.

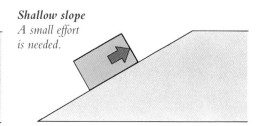

Steep slope
A large effort is needed.

Shallow slope
A small effort is needed.

Shallow and steep
On a steep slope, all the work is done in a short distance and needs a large effort. On a gentle slope, the work is done over a much longer distance, making it easier.

Ramps for building
This picture was copied from an ancient Egyptian tomb painting and shows a ramp being used to construct a building. Without construction machines such as cranes, the Egyptians had to build huge sloping ramps to pull stone blocks to the upper levels of the building.

Fast track

When engineers plan roads such as motorways, they try to avoid having a steep carriageway. Cuttings and embankments are built into hillsides. Vehicles can climb the gentle slopes without slowing down too much.

Mountain roads

Mountain roads, such as this one in South Africa, zigzag upwards in a series of gentle slopes. A road straight up the side of the valley would be far too steep for most vehicles to drive up.

Access ramps

This man is using a ramp to get down to the beach. Ramps make it much easier for wheels to reach from one level to another. Many public buildings, such as libraries, sports centres and hospitals, often have ramps leading up to their doors as well as steps. Without ramps, people with wheelchairs or push-chairs often find it very difficult to get in and out of a building.

FACT BOX

• Most canals have flights of locks to move boats up and down hill, but a few use inclined planes, or ramps. In a 1.6 km long inclined plane in Belgium, the boats float inside huge 5,000 tonne tanks of water. The tanks are hauled up the inclined plane on rails.

• The railway line from Lima to Galera, in Peru, climbs 4,780 m. In some places the track zigzags backwards and forwards across the very steep hillsides.

WEDGES AND SCREWS

WEDGES and screw threads are simple machines that use inclined planes, or ramps, to work. Think of a wedge as two ramps, back-to-back. Pushing the thin end of a wedge into a narrow gap with a small effort makes the wedge press hard on the edges of the gap, forcing the gap apart. Chisels, axes and ploughs all work with wedges. If you look at their blades you will see that they widen from the edge.

Screw threads are also a type of inclined plane. If you imagine a long, narrow ramp wrapped around a pole, you end up with a screw thread. Screw threads make screws, nuts and bolts, bench vices and car jacks work. Turning the screw thread with a small effort makes it move in or out with great force. Screw threads provide a very secure way of fixing something together, or of raising a heavy load.

A door wedge stops a door opening or closing. Pulling on the door makes the wedge press even harder against the bottom of the door and the floor.

Wedges as cutters
An axe head is wedge-shaped. When it hits the wood, its sharp edge sinks in, forcing the wood apart and splitting it. The handle allows the person operating the axe to swing it with great speed and lever out pieces of wood.

Wedge strippers
This forestry worker is using a wedge-shaped tool to split the bark from a tree trunk. The sharp edge is a shallow slope that cuts and lifts the bark in one movement.

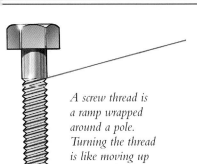

A screw thread is a ramp wrapped around a pole. Turning the thread is like moving up or down the slope.

A spiralling slope

A corkscrew has a screw thread that makes it wind into a cork as the handle is turned. The screw only moves a small way into the cork for each turn of the handle. This makes winding the corkscrew quite easy.

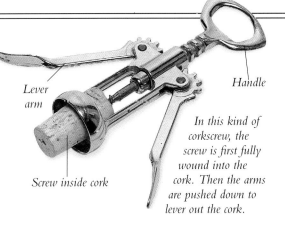

Lever arm

Handle

Screw inside cork

In this kind of corkscrew, the screw is first fully wound into the cork. Then the arms are pushed down to lever out the cork.

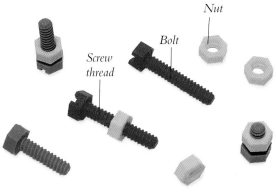

Nut

Bolt

Screw thread

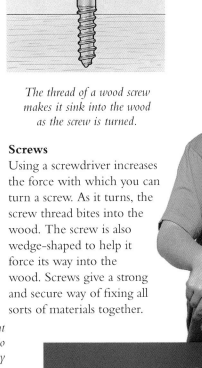

The thread of a wood screw makes it sink into the wood as the screw is turned.

Nuts and bolts

Nuts and bolts make a firm joint. The screw thread on a bolt forces the nut on to the bolt when the two are turned together with a spanner. Turning the nut forces it tightly on to the head of the bolt, pulling the joint together.

Screws

Using a screwdriver increases the force with which you can turn a screw. As it turns, the screw thread bites into the wood. The screw is also wedge-shaped to help it force its way into the wood. Screws give a strong and secure way of fixing all sorts of materials together.

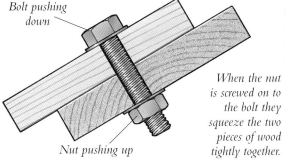

Bolt pushing down

When the nut is screwed on to the bolt they squeeze the two pieces of wood tightly together.

Nut pushing up

PLANES AT WORK

You will need: piece of wooden board or thick card, long bolt with a nut and washer to fit, strong glue, lolly stick or short piece of wood, cardboard tube, card, a weight to lift.

Ramps, wedges and screw threads are all adaptations of the inclined plane. The inclined plane is a lifting device and, although screw threads are most commonly used for joining things together, another important application for the screw is the screw jack. Instead of the force made by turning the screw thread creating a tight grip, it is used to lift a weight upwards. With a screw jack, a huge weight, such as a car, can be lifted easily, but slowly. The first project on these pages shows you how to make a simple type of screw jack. The second project shows you how to make a device to measure force, or the effort needed to raise an object. Use it to compare how a gentler slope makes lifting an object easier.

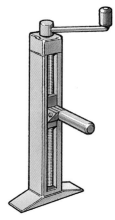

Most cars carry a screw jack inside. If the car gets a puncture, the driver can lift the car with the jack before changing the wheel.

Make a screw jack

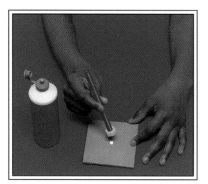

1 Find a square piece of wooden board or thick card. Glue the head of the long bolt to the middle of the square so that the thread is pointing upwards. Leave to dry.

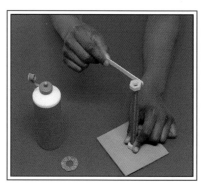

2 Glue the end of the lolly stick to the side of the nut (the nut must fit the bolt) to make a handle. When the glue is dry, wind the nut on to the bolt and put the washer on top.

3 Stick the tube to a rectangle of card. Place tube over the bolt so it rests on top of the washer. Move a weight up and down by turning the handle on the nut.

MATERIALS

You will need: piece of wood or thick card, elastic band, paper fastener, string, pencil or felt tip pen, ruler, model vehicle.

Measuring the forces on a slope

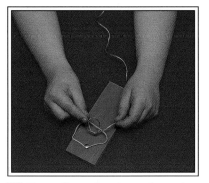

1 You will need a piece of wood or card about 15 cm x 5 cm. Attach the elastic band near one end with a paper fastener. Tie a piece of string to the other end of the band.

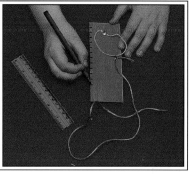

2 Mark a simple scale on the wood or card. Use it to record how far the elastic band stretches to when it is pulled by the weight. You have now made your force measurer.

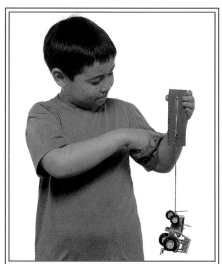

3 Use your force measurer to find the weight of the model vehicle. Hang the model from your measurer and note where the band stretches to. Write down the measurement.

4 Make a slope – try using a plank propped up on books. How much force is needed to pull the vehicle up the slope? Is it less or greater than the model's weight? Try again with a shallower slope. Does the force needed change? You should see that it needs less force to pull the model vehicle up the shallower slope.

PULLEYS

A pulley is a form of another simple machine, the wheel and axle. The simplest pulley system is a wheel with a groove in its rim in which a rope is fitted. The wheel rotates around an axle. The rope hangs down either side of the wheel, with one end attached to a load. Pulling down on the rope lifts the load hanging on the other end. This simple system does not reduce the amount of force needed to lift an object, so there is no mechanical advantage. It does, however, make lifting the load easier, because it is easier to pull down than it is to pull up. A pulley's special advantage is that it changes the direction of the force or effort. Using several pulleys together makes lifting even easier and many pulley systems have more than one pulley wheel. A pulley system like this is called a block and tackle. Pulleys are useful for lifting loads on building sites and for moving heavy parts and machinery in factories.

A simple pulley changes the direction of the effort needed to lift a load off the ground. Instead of pulling up, this boy pulls down.

Pulleys for building

In this picture from the 1500s, workmen are using a pulley to lift building materials. They are using it to construct the walls of a great city. The workman at the bottom turns a handle to haul up the bucket. The pulley was probably first used in Greece about 2,500 years ago and has been in use ever since.

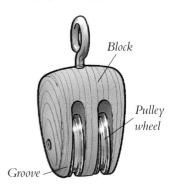

Block

Pulley wheel

Groove

A block and tackle has two blocks like the one shown above, arranged one above the other. The pulley wheels are designed to turn easily as the rope runs around them, through the groove.

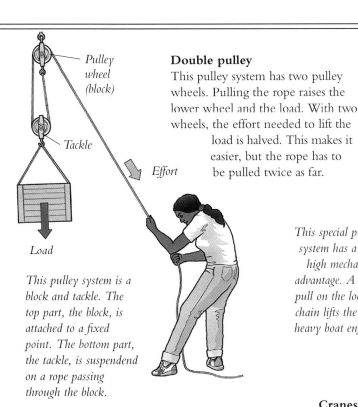

Pulley wheel (block)

Tackle

Effort

Load

This pulley system is a block and tackle. The top part, the block, is attached to a fixed point. The bottom part, the tackle, is suspendend on a rope passing through the block.

Double pulley

This pulley system has two pulley wheels. Pulling the rope raises the lower wheel and the load. With two wheels, the effort needed to lift the load is halved. This makes it easier, but the rope has to be pulled twice as far.

This special pulley system has a very high mechanical advantage. A light pull on the loop of chain lifts the very heavy boat engine.

Cranes

Cranes use pulley systems to lift heavy loads. On this dock crane you can see the steel lifting cables running along the crane's arm.

Pulleys are used to quickly raise and lower lifeboats on board a ship. Pulleys are also used on sailing boats, for example, to raise and lower the sails.

PULLEYS AT WORK

THE two projects on these pages illustrate how pulley systems work. In the first project, a simple double pulley system is constructed. It does not have pulley wheels. Instead, the string passes over smooth metal hoops. Metal hoops are not as efficient as pulley wheels, but they will show you how a pulley system is connected. The second project investigates how adding more turns on a block and tackle reduces the effort needed to move a load. You will probably notice, however, that the more turns you make, the greater the friction becomes. Using wheels in a block and tackle cuts down this friction.

Heavy-duty block and tackle systems, like this one in a dockyard, have metal chain links. These are much stronger than a rope would be. The chain links interlock with the shaped pulley wheels.

Make a simple pulley

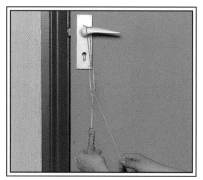

1 Take a short length of string. Use the string to tie a large paper clip to a door handle, or another support off the floor. Make sure the paper clip is tied securely to its support.

2 Cut a long piece of string and feed it through the paper clip's inner hoop. Now feed it through the top of a second paper clip and tie it to the outer hoop of the top clip.

3 Fix a weight, using another piece of string, to the bottom paper clip. Pull the end of the long string to lift the bottom paper clip, which will lift the weight.

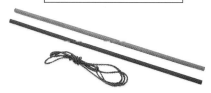

You will need:
two broom handles or lengths
of thick dowelling, strong string
or thin rope, two friends.

Make a block and tackle

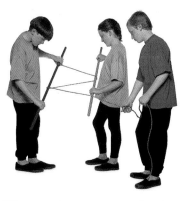

1 Ask each of your friends to hold a broom handle, or length of dowelling, between outstretched hands. Tie the end of a long piece of string, or rope, to one of the handles.

2 Wrap the string around each handle once, keeping the loops fairly close together on the handles. Now pull on the string. How easy was it to pull your friends together?

3 Now wrap the string twice around each handle, making sure to keep the turns close together. Now pull on the end of the string again. What differences do you notice this time? Is it any easier?

4 Make more turns around the handles and try pulling again. Do more turns make the effort you need to make smaller? Do you have to pull the rope farther than before?

GEAR WHEELS

A gear is a wheel with teeth around its edge. When two gear wheels are put next to each other their teeth can be made to interlock. This means that turning one wheel makes the other wheel turn, too. Gears are used to transmit movement from one wheel to another. If both wheels are the same size, the wheels turn at the same speed. If one wheel is bigger than the other, the gears can be used to speed up or slow down movement, or to increase or decrease a force. Many different machines, from kitchen whisks to massive trucks, have gears that help them to work. Belt drives and chain drives are similar to gears. In these, two wheels are linked together by a belt or a chain instead of teeth. This is another way of transferring power and movement from one shaft to another. Speed can also be varied by changing the size of the wheels.

This is a simple gear system. One gear wheel turns the other because the teeth interlock with each other. The bigger wheel will also make the smaller wheel turn faster because it is twice the size of the smaller one.

Transmitting a force
In the centre of this kitchen whisk is a set of gears. They are used to transmit the turning movement of the handle to the blades of the whisk. The gears speed up the movement, making the blades spin faster than the turning handle.

Turning handle

Cover protecting small gear wheels

Drive wheel

Shaft

Blades

The drive wheel transmits the motion of the handle to the smaller gear wheels attached to the shafts. The smaller gears turn much faster than the larger drive wheel and in the opposite direction to each other.

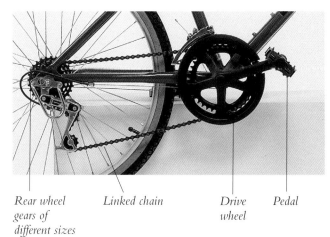

Rear wheel gears of different sizes   Linked chain   Drive wheel   Pedal

Bicycle gears

Bicycle gears use wheels and a chain to transmit the drive from the pedals to the bicycle's rear wheel. As a rider turns the pedals, the drive wheel is moved around. This moves a linked chain, which turns a gear wheel attached to the rear wheel. Moving the chain to another larger or smaller gear wheel changes how many times the rear wheel turns for each turn of the pedals. This affects the bike's speed, helping it to go faster.

Watch gears

The back has been removed from this wind-up watch so you can see the tiny gear wheels inside. Different-sized gear wheels are arranged so that they move the hands of the watch at different speeds. The clock is powered by a spring, wound up by hand. The spring makes a gear wheel turn, which moves the minute hand. Another gear slows down this movement to turn the hour hand.

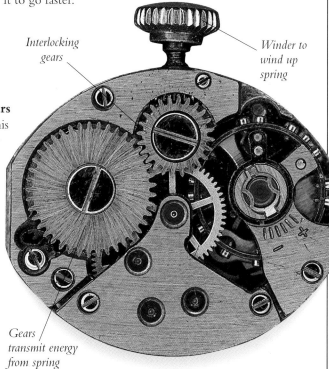

Interlocking gears

Winder to wind up spring

Gears transmit energy from spring

Belt drives

This picture of a factory was taken in about 1905. It shows wide belts stretching between wheels in the roof and the machines. These are belt drives. The wheels in the roof are turned by an engine, and the belts transmit this movement to drive the machines.

MAKING GEARS WORK

You will need: compass and pencil, protractor, thick card, scissors, used matchsticks or thin dowelling, glue, paper fasteners, small cardboard box.

B EFORE engineers started using metals, they made gear wheels from wood. One way of making gear-wheel teeth was to fix short wooden poles on to the edge of a thick wooden disc. The poles on different gear wheels interlocked to transmit movement. Gears like this were being used 2,000 years ago. If you visit an old mill, you might still see similar wooden gears today. The first project on these pages shows you how to make a simple gear wheel system. When you have made it, what do you notice about how the wheels turn? They will turn in different directions and the smaller wheel, with fewer teeth, will turn one and a half times for every one rotation of the larger wheel. The second project shows you how to make a simple belt drive and how it can turn an axle at different speeds.

3 Use paper fasteners to attach one wheel to the top of the box and the other to the side so that the teeth interlock. Turn one disc to turn the other.

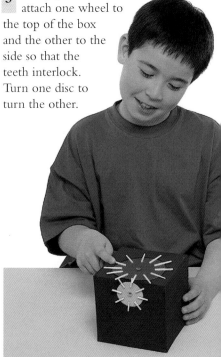

Make a set of gear wheels

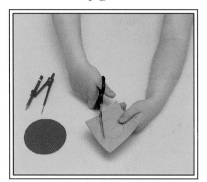

1 Using a pencil and compass, mark out two discs on card and cut them out. Make the diameter of one disc twice the diameter of the other, for example 8 cm and 4 cm.

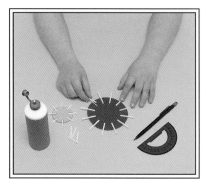

2 Glue eight matches around the edge of the small disc. First glue four matches in a cross shape, then add four more half-way. In a similar way, glue 12 matches to the large disc.

Make a belt drive

1 You will need two pieces of dowelling each about 5 cm longer than the width of the box. Cut a pair of holes in both sides of the box. Slide the rods through to make two axles.

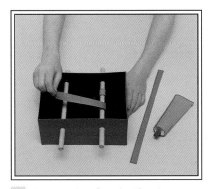

2 Cut a strip of card. Glue it to one of the axles. Wrap it round and glue the end down to make a wheel. Make a bigger wheel with a strip of card three times longer than the first.

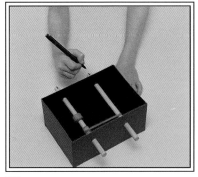

3 Put a wide elastic band around both axles. The band should be slightly stretched when it is in place. Make a mark at the end of each axle so you can see how fast they turn.

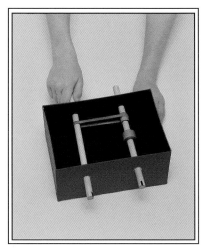

4 To test your belt drive, put the elastic band on to the smaller wheel and start turning the plain axle. Does the wheeled axle turn more or fewer times than the plain?

M A T E R I A L S

You will need: cardboard box, dowelling, scissors, strips of thin card, glue, thick elastic band, felt tip pen.

5 Now move the elastic band on to the larger wheel and start turning the plain axle again. What difference does it make to the speed of the wheeled axle? Use the pen marks to compare the speeds.

POWER FOR MACHINES

THE first machines, such as axes and ramps, relied on human muscle power to make them work. Then people started using animals to work many simple machines. Animals can carry, pull and lift much heavier loads than people can. Eventually people realized they could capture the energy of the wind and flowing water by using windmills and water-wheels. These were the first machines built to create power to make other machines work. This energy was in the form of movement energy and it was used to do such things as grinding grain to make flour or pumping up water from underground. Today, wind and water energy are still captured, but they are used to make electricity, which we use to light and power our homes, schools, offices and factories.

Windmills like this one were used to capture the energy of the wind to grind grain. The whole building can be turned round so that the sails point into the wind.

Overshot water-wheel

There are two different types of water-wheel. This one is called an overshot wheel. The water flows along the channel above the wheel and falls into the buckets. The water's weight pulls the wheel around.

Undershot water-wheel

This picture shows the second type of water-wheel, called an undershot wheel. The rushing water in a stream or river is harnessed when it catches in the buckets at the bottom of the wheel. The force of the water spins the wheel.

Grinding stones

Many wind and water-mills make power to turn millstones. The grinding stones in this picture are used to squeeze oil from olives. Only the top millstone turns while the bottom stone stays still.

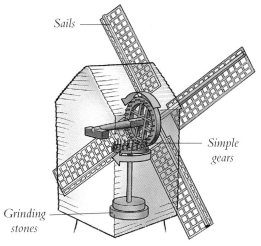

This picture shows the inside of a windmill. The arrangement of wooden gear wheels transfers power from the sails to the grinding stones. Mills like this have been in use for centuries.

Sails

Simple gears

Grinding stones

Hydroelectrity

A hydroelectric station makes electricity from flowing water. The water is stored behind a huge dam. As it flows out, it spins a turbine, which is like a very efficient water-wheel. The turbine turns a generator to make electricity.

Wind turbines

Wind turbines, like these shown on a wind farm, are a modern type of windmill. The wind spins the huge propellers, which turns an electricity generator inside the top of each turbine.

WIND AND WATER POWER

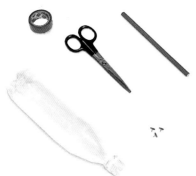

You will need:
plastic bottle, scissors, sticky
tape, thin dowelling,
drawing pins.

MODERN windmills are called wind turbines and are used to generate electricity. The most efficient wind turbines only have two or three blades, like the propeller of an aircraft. Hundreds of small wind turbines can be grouped together to make a wind farm. In other places, one or two large turbines generate enough electricity to power a small community. There are several shapes of wind turbine, but one of the most efficient is the vertical-axis turbine. It is called this because its axle is vertical to the ground. The first project shows you how to make a vertical-axis turbine. It is very efficient because it works no matter which way the wind is blowing. The second project shows you how to make an overshot water-wheel. This captures the energy of falling water to lift a small weight. Try pouring the water on to the wheel from different heights to see if it makes a difference to the wheel's speed.

Make a windmill

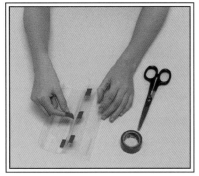

1 Cut the top and bottom off the bottle to leave a tube. Cut the tube in half to make two curved vanes. Stick the vanes together with the edges overlapping by about 2 cm.

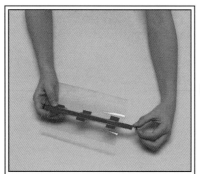

2 The piece of dowelling should be about 4 cm longer than the vanes. Slide it into the slot between the vanes. Press a drawing pin gently into each end of the dowelling.

3 Hold the turbine in a loose grip and blow on the vanes. It will spin easily.

Make a water-wheel

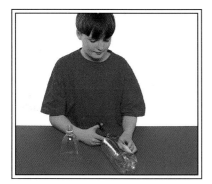

1 Cut the top third off the plastic bottle. Cut a small hole in the bottom piece near the base (this is to let the water out). Cut a V-shape on each side of the rim.

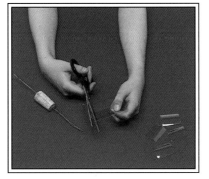

2 Ask an adult to push the wire through the centre of the cork to make an axle. From the top third of the plastic bottle, cut six small curved vanes as shown.

3 Ask an adult to cut six slots in the cork with a craft knife. (This might be easier without the wire.) Push the plastic vanes into the slots to make the water-wheel.

4 Rest the wheel's axle in the V-shaped slots. Tape a length of string towards one end of the axle and tie a small weight to the end of the string. Fill a jug with water.

MATERIALS

You will need: large plastic bottle, scissors, wire (ask an adult to cut the bottom out of a coat hanger), cork, craft knife, sticky tape, string, weight, jug of water, large plate.

5 Put the water-wheel on a large plate or in the sink. Pour water on to the wheel so that it hits the upward-curving vanes. The weight should be lifted up.

ENGINES AND MOTORS

MANY modern machines get the power they need to work from engines and motors. Engines and motors are complicated machines themselves. An engine is a machine that makes movement energy from heat. The heat is made by burning a fuel, such as petrol. The first engines were driven by steam. Most engines today, such as the ones used in cars, are internal combustion engines. This means that the fuel is burned inside the engine. In a car engine, as the petrol explodes, it produces hot gases that push pistons inside cylinders up and down. The pistons turn a crankshaft, which carries the movement energy from the engine to the wheels of the car. An electric motor is a machine that makes movement energy from electricity rather than from burning fuel. Most of the electricity we use is made in power stations or from the chemicals inside batteries.

This is a portable generator. It is made up of a small internal combustion engine that is used to turn an electricity generator. Powered by petrol or diesel, generators are useful where there is no mains electricity, or if there is a break in the supply.

Steam power

This locomotive is powered by steam. Steam was the main form of power in the 1800s. Steam engines are called external combustion engines, because the fuel burns outside the cylinders.

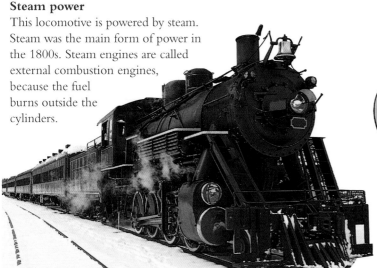

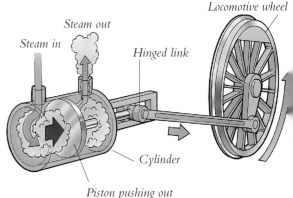

Steam out

Steam in

Locomotive wheel

Hinged link

Cylinder

Piston pushing out

In a steam engine, steam made by heating water in a boiler is forced along a pipe into a cylinder. The pressure of the steam pushes a piston in the cylinder outwards. The moving piston then turns a wheel that is used to drive a locomotive or power a machine.

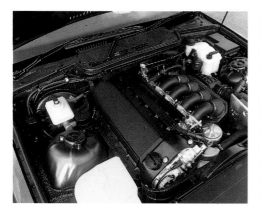

Engines for cars

Under the bonnet of a car is an internal combustion engine. In this picture, the engine's cylinders are inside the large black engine block. You can see the exhaust pipes that carry away waste gases from the cylinders.

Jet engines

Fast aircraft, such as this military fighter, have jet engines. A jet engine creates a fast-moving stream of hot gases. These shoot out the back of the engine and push the aircraft forwards.

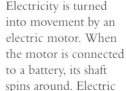

Electric motors

Electricity is turned into movement by an electric motor. When the motor is connected to a battery, its shaft spins around. Electric motors are small and clean, which makes them useful for household gadgets.

An electric motor with a colourful spinner on top is connected to a battery by two wires. This makes an electric circuit.

Spinner

Battery

Wire

Motor

HYDRAULICS AND PNEUMATICS

Not all machines have parts that are moved by engines or motors. Hydraulic machines have parts moved by a liquid and pneumatic machines have parts moved by a gas. A simple hydraulic system has a pipe filled with oil and a piston fitted at each end. Pushing one piston into the pipe forces the piston at the other end outwards, transmitting power from one end of the pipe to the other. In a simple pneumatic system, compressed air is used to force a piston to move.

Hydraulic and pneumatic machines can be very powerful. They are also quite simple and very robust. Machines that work in dirty and rough conditions, such as diggers, drills and tipper trucks, often have hydraulic or pneumatic systems instead of motors. Most dental drills are also worked by a pneumatic system. Air, pumped to the drill, makes a tiny turbine inside the drill spin very fast. It is the air escaping from the drill that makes the high-pitched whine.

This girl is lifting the book with pneumatic power. She is blowing air into the inflated balloon and pushing the book upwards. Less effort is needed to lift the book like this than is needed to lift it by hand.

Pumping air

All pneumatic machines need a device to suck in air from the outside and push it into the machine. This is called an air pump, or compressor. The simple air pump below sucks in air as the piston is pulled back and forces air out as the piston is pushed in.

Using an air pump is a simple way to blow up a balloon. A valve in the pump's outlet allows air to be pumped into the balloon as the piston is pushed in. It prevents the air being sucked out again when the piston is pulled out.

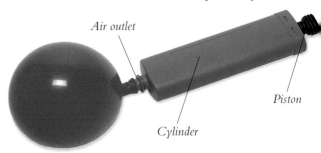

Air outlet

Piston

Cylinder

Hydraulic lift
Lifting a heavy load is easy with an hydraulic machine like this fork-lift truck. Hydraulic rams create the lifting force. Each ram consists of a cylinder and piston. Pumping oil, or hydraulic fluid, into the cylinder makes the piston move out or in.

This simple hydraulic system has two pistons connected by a cylinder filled with hydraulic fluid. Using different sized pistons creates a mechanical advantage. Pushing the small piston creates a greater force at the large piston.

Large piston is pushed out a short way but with greater force

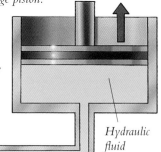

Hydraulic fluid

Small piston is pushed in a long way with little force

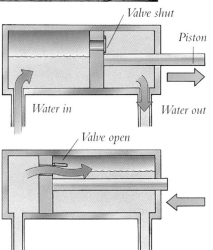

Valve shut

Piston

Water in

Water out

Valve open

Pumping water
Moving this water pump's piston in and out moves water from the pipe on the left to the pipe on the right. The valve opens to let water through as the piston moves in. The valve shuts automatically as the piston moves out because the water presses it closed.

Pneumatic drill
Pneumatic drills are used to break through hard surfaces. Here, you can see the pipe leading from the air compressor to the drill. The drill works more like a hammer, as its blade strikes the surface with great force.

LIQUID AND AIR AT WORK

You will need: large plastic bottle, scissors, airtight plastic bag, plastic tubing, sticky tape, plastic funnel, spray can lid, heavy weight, jug of water.

HYDRAULIC machinery uses a liquid to transmit power, while pneumatic machinery uses compressed air. The first project shows you how to make a simple hydraulic machine that uses water pressure to lift an object upwards. A central reservoir (a jug of water) is poured into a pipe. The water fills up a plastic bag, which is forced to expand in a narrow cylinder. This forces up a platform, which in turn raises a heavy object. Many cranes, excavators and trucks use this principle to lift heavy loads, using hydraulic rams.

The second project shows you how to make a simple air pump. An air pump works by sucking air in one hole and pushing it out of another. A valve stops the air being sucked in and pushed out of the wrong holes. When the air tries to flow through one way, the valve opens, but when the air tries to flow through the other way it stays shut.

Make an hydraulic lifter

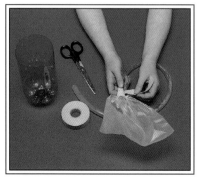

1 Cut the top off the large plastic bottle. Make sure the plastic bag is airtight and wrap its neck over the end of a length of plastic tubing. Seal the bag to the tube with tape.

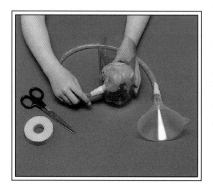

2 Fix a funnel to the other end of the tube. Make a hole at the base of the bottle and feed the bag and tubing through. The bag should sit in the bottom of the bottle.

3 Put the spray can lid on top of the bag and rest a book, or another heavy object, on top of the bottle. Lift the funnel end of the tubing up, and slowly pour in water. What happens to the can lid and the book?

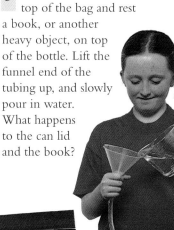

Make an air pump

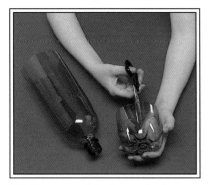

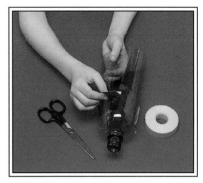

1 Cut around the large plastic bottle, about one third up from the bottom. Cut a slit down the side of the bottom part of the bottle so that it will slide inside the top part.

2 Ask an adult to help you nail the bottom of the bottle to the end of a wooden stick or piece of dowelling. You have now made a piston for your air pump.

3 Cut a hole about 1 cm across near the neck of the bottle. Cut a piece of card about 2 cm x 2 cm. Tape one edge of the card to the bottle to form a flap over the hole.

MATERIALS

You will need: large plastic bottle, scissors, hammer, small nails, wooden stick or dowelling, card, sticky tape, table tennis ball.

4 Drop a table tennis ball into the top part of the bottle so that it rests in the neck. Push the bottom part of the bottle (the piston) into the top part (the cylinder).

5 Move the piston in and out to suck air into the bottle and out of the hole. Can you see how both the valves work? The flap should automatically close when you pull the piston out.

MACHINES AT HOME

THE average home is full of machines. Look in the kitchen, the bathroom, the living room and bedroom. In your kitchen you should find several simple gadgets, such as can openers, taps, scissors and bottle openers. There might also be more complicated machines, such as a washing machine or a dishwasher. Other machines you might find include a vacuum cleaner and a hairdryer. Even the zips on your clothes are machines. Think about how each one might save you time and effort. What would life be like without them? Most machines not only save you work, but also improve the results – a modern washing machine get clothes far cleaner than an old-fashioned tub. Many of these machines need electricity to work and are powered from the mains supply.

Zip fastener

One of the simplest machines is the zip. If you look carefully at the zip fastener, you will see a wedge shape in the middle. This forces the two edges of the zip together to do it up, and apart again to undo it.

Wheel and axle

Lever arm

Wedge

Can opener
Can you see four different types of machine in a can opener? You should be able to find levers, a wedge, a wheel and axle and a gear wheel. Together, they make it simple to open a can.

FACT BOX
• The zip was invented in 1893. The first zips were unreliable until tiny bumps and hollows were added to the end of each tooth.

• Electrically powered domestic machines were only possible once mains electricity was developed in the 1880s.

• One of the earliest vacuum cleaners was built in 1901. It was so large that it was pulled by a horse and powered by a petrol engine.

• The idea of the spin dryer was thought of by a French engineer in 1865, but it was not used until the 1920s.

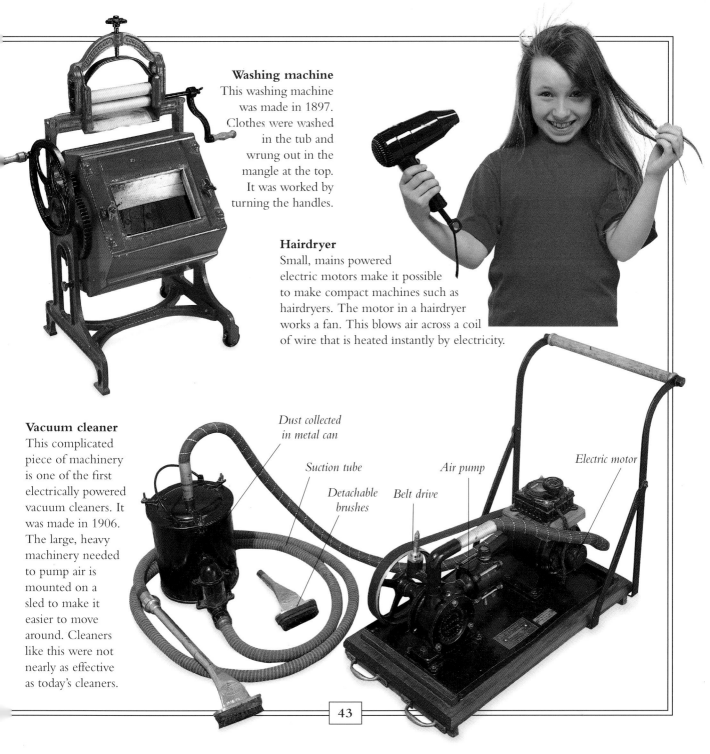

Washing machine

This washing machine was made in 1897. Clothes were washed in the tub and wrung out in the mangle at the top. It was worked by turning the handles.

Hairdryer

Small, mains powered electric motors make it possible to make compact machines such as hairdryers. The motor in a hairdryer works a fan. This blows air across a coil of wire that is heated instantly by electricity.

Vacuum cleaner

This complicated piece of machinery is one of the first electrically powered vacuum cleaners. It was made in 1906. The large, heavy machinery needed to pump air is mounted on a sled to make it easier to move around. Cleaners like this were not nearly as effective as today's cleaners.

Dust collected in metal can

Suction tube

Detachable brushes

Belt drive

Air pump

Electric motor

MAKING DOMESTIC MACHINES

M A T E R I A L S

You will need:
two short planks of wood,
hinge, screws, screwdriver, two
coffee-jar lids, glue.

THE simple domestic, or household, machines on these pages are easy to make. They are a can crusher and a hand-operated vacuum cleaner. Use the can crusher to flatten empty drinks cans before you take them for recycling or to the tip. Crushed cans take up far less space than empty, full-sized ones. This makes them easier to store and to carry. The crusher is a simple machine that uses a lever action to press on the ends of the can. It is much easier to crush a can with the machine than it is with your hands. The vacuum cleaner is based on the air pump, instructions for which can be found on page 41. It uses the same principles to pick up bits of paper as a more sophisticated vacuum cleaner does to pick up household dust. Tissue paper is used for the collection bag because it allows air to pass through it and filters out the bits of paper. Securing the table tennis ball to the neck of the pump makes the cleaner more efficient, as it prevents the ball from falling too far out of place.

Make a can crusher

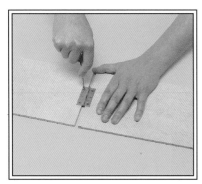

1 Find two planks of wood, about 50 cm x 10 cm and 1–2 cm thick. Lay the two planks end to end and ask an adult to help you join them together with a hinge.

2 Glue a jar lid to each plank of wood with the top of the lid face down. The lids should be about half-way along each plank and the same distance from the hinge.

3 To crush a can, put the can in between the lids so that it is held in place. Press on the top piece of wood.

MATERIALS

You will need: large plastic bottle, scissors, hammer, small nails, wooden stick or dowelling, table tennis ball, string, sticky tape, tissue paper, glue.

Make a vacuum cleaner

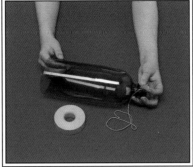

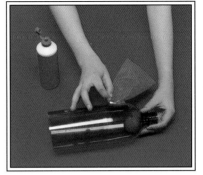

1 Make the air pump (see page 41) but leave off the card valve. Tape a length of string to the ball. Feed the string through the neck of the bottle. Tape the string to the neck so that it only allows the ball to fall a few millimetres out of the neck.

2 Make a tissue paper bag and glue it over the hole in the bottle. Air from the pump will go through the bag and anything the vacuum picks up should be trapped.

Modern vacuum cleaners have a powerful air pump powered by an electric motor. The pump sucks air up through a tube and into a collection bag.

3 Try picking up tiny bits of paper with the vacuum. Pull the piston out sharply to suck the bits of paper into the bottle. Push the piston back in gently to pump the paper into the tissue bag. How much can you pick up with your home-made cleaner? Can you think of a way to improve it?

TRANSPORT MACHINES

BICYCLES, cars, buses, trucks, trains, ships and aircraft are all transport machines. They all make it easier and quicker to travel from one place to another by making wide use of different types of engines, motors, gears and wheels. The bicycle is one of the most complicated machines that relies on human muscle power to work. A bicycle includes several types of simple machine and is designed to reduce effort to a minimum. Larger transport machines have engines and motors to power them. Many also make use of hydraulic, pneumatic and electronic systems. The different systems combine together to make the machine efficient and safe.

The first bicycles had no gears and no pedals. They were called hobbyhorses and the rider had to push one along the ground with his or her feet. Even so, they were still quicker than walking.

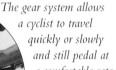

The gear system allows a cyclist to travel quickly or slowly and still pedal at a comfortable rate.

On your bicycle

A cyclist uses her energy to push the pedals. The gear system uses this push to turn the back wheel and drive the bike forwards. Air hitting her body, her weight and friction between the tyres and the road all try to slow her down.

Tyres and air

A pump is used to pump air into the tyres. A valve in the tyre lets air in, but stops it escaping. Tyres are pumped full of air to give a smoother, easier ride.

The brake lever on the handlebar pulls a cable that makes a brake block press on the wheel rim.

Electric trains

The fastest trains, such as this French TGV, are moved by powerful electric motors. The electricity comes from overhead cables above the track.

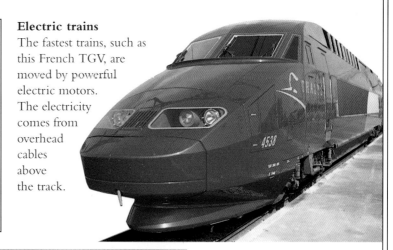

Cars

All modern cars, from sports cars to small family cars, have similar parts. They are moved by an internal combustion engine that burns petrol or diesel fuel. The brakes are worked hydraulically.

Aircraft

Airliners, such as this Airbus A340, are the most complex transport machines. They are able to carry 300 or more passengers at one time. Airliners are driven by powerful jet engines and use hydraulic systems to control their flight. Safety is very important in air travel, so most of the aircraft's systems have back-up systems in case something goes wrong.

BUILDING MACHINES

CONSTRUCTING houses, office blocks, bridges, roads and railways involves digging into the ground, moving rock and earth, and transporting and lifting steel, concrete and other heavy building materials. There are specialized construction machines, such as diggers, bulldozers, concrete mixers and cranes, to carry out all these jobs. Many of them use the principles of simple machines to work. For example, cranes use pulleys and balanced levers to help them lift. Most construction machines have large diesel engines to provide the power they need, and some have hydraulic or pneumatic systems to move their parts.

This picture is called The Tower of Babel *and was painted by Pieter Brueghel in 1563. It shows the machines people used to build with. There are chisels, levers, pulleys and even cranes operated by huge treadmills.*

Earth mover
A bulldozer is used to push rock, soil and rubble away to clear a building site ready for work to start. Its wide tracks, called caterpillar tracks, stop it sinking into muddy ground.

Digging out
This mechanical excavator is used to dig up rock and soil. It makes trenches for pipes and holes for foundations. Its powerful digging arm is moved by hydraulic rams.

Moving mixer

This lorry is a concrete mixer. It carries concrete to the building site from the factory. Inside the drum a blade, like a screw thread, mixes the concrete. The blade stays still while the drum rotates.

Hammering in

This pile driver hammers piles, or metal posts, into the ground. It repeatedly lifts a large weight with its crane and drops it on to the top of the pile. The piles form the foundation of a new building.

Towering crane

These tower cranes look flimsy, but they do not topple over even when they are lifting heavy weights. This is because of a concrete counterweight behind the cab.

FACT BOX
• A tower crane can build itself by increasing the height of its tower. The crane is hauled up and a new section of tower is lifted into place.

• Tunnels that go through soft rock, such as chalk, are dug with tunnel boring machines. The machine bores its way through the rock with a rotating cutting head.

• The Romans used cranes to build with around 2,000 years ago. They were powered by slaves walking round in a giant treadmill.

Tipping out

Dumper trucks are used to deliver hardcore (crushed up stones used for foundations) and to take away unwanted soil. To empty it, the body is tipped up by hydraulic rams.

ON THE FARM

Some of the oldest types of machines in the world are agricultural machines. Farmers use machines to prepare the soil, to sow and harvest their crops, and to feed and milk their animals. One of the first, and still one of the most important farm machines, was the plough. Archaeologists have found evidence of ploughs from about 9,000 years ago. They began as a simple, sharpened stick that was used to turn up the soil. Today, a seven-furrow plough hauled behind a modern tractor can cover 40 hectares of land in a day. Modern farming uses many specialized machines to make cultivated land more productive. In some parts of the world, powered machinery, usually operated by a tractor, does all the work. But in many countries, ploughs are pulled by animals and crops are harvested using simple hand tools.

The spade is a simple machine for lifting and turning soil. A sharp blade makes it easy to push into the soil. Pulling on the handle levers soil up.

Steam power
Steam-driven traction engines were the first type of tractor. This one was built in 1880. It replaced the farm's horses and powered other machines, such as the thresher shown here.

Animal power
This water buffalo is pulling a plough through the soil. Animals, especially oxen, are still widely used by farmers who cannot afford machines or who live in hilly areas.

Tractor and plough

Modern, tractor-pulled ploughs have several individual ploughs in a row to break up the soil into furrows. This makes it much quicker to plough a field than with a single plough.

Combine harvester

A combine harvester cuts and collects crops. A reel sweeps the crop into a cutter bar that slices the stalks off at ground level. It is then pushed into the machine where the grain is stripped from the stalks.

FACT BOX

• Combine harvesters often use screws to move the grain around inside the harvester. These are called impeller screws, or augers.

• At the rear end of a tractor is a rotating shaft called a take-off shaft. It provides power for machines that the tractor is pulling.

• One of the most important argicultural inventions was the seed drill, which planted seeds in neat rows and at the correct depth.

Milking parlour
Cow's milk is pumped from the udders to a container where it is weighed and measured. The milk is then pumped to a refrigerated tank ready to be collected by a lorry.

MAKING FARM MACHINES

Inside an Archimedean screw is a wide screw thread. Water is trapped in the thread and is forced to move upwards as the screw is turned. A screw thread like this is also called an auger.

THE two projects on these pages will show you how to make two simple farm machines. The first is an Archimedean screw. In parts of the world where water pumps are expensive to buy and run, Archimedean screws are used to move water uphill in order to irrigate crops. The machine is made up of a large screw inside a pipe. One end of the machine is placed in the water and, as a handle is turned, the screw inside revolves, carrying water upwards. This water-lifting device has been in use for centuries and it is named after the ancient Greek scientist, Archimedes. The second project is to make a simple plough. By pushing it through a tray of damp sand you will be able to see how the special curved shape of a real plough lifts and turns the soil to make a furrow.

M A T E R I A L S

You will need: small plastic bottle, scissors, plastic tubing, waterproof sticky tape, two bowls.

Make an Archimedean screw

1 Cut the top and bottom off the bottle. Wrap a length of plastic tubing around the bottle to make a screw thread shape. Tape the tubing in place with waterproof sticky tape.

2 Put one end of the bottle in a bowl of water and rest the bottle on the bowl's edge. Slowly turn the bottle. After a few turns, the water will start to pour out of the top end of the tubing.

Make a simple plough

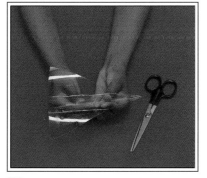

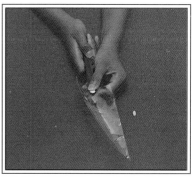

1 Start by cutting a triangle of plastic from one side of the small plastic drinks bottle. This triangle will form the blade of your plough.

2 Cut a slot in the triangle, as shown above. Fold the triangle in half along the line of the slot against the curve of the plastic.

3 Fix the blade to the length of wood or dowelling with a drawing pin. Make sure the blade is securely attatched to the handle.

You will need: small plastic bottle, scissors, strip of wood or dowelling, drawing pin, tray of damp sand.

4 Fill up the tray with damp sand and push the plough through the sand in lines. Does your plough lift and turn the soil to make a furrow?

This picture shows a wheeled plough from the 1400s. It has a specially shaped wooden frame and an iron blade. The farmer guides the plough while a helper urges on two oxen and two horses.

ELECTRONIC MACHINES

Most of the machines we use everyday have moving parts that are operated by hand or by an engine or motor. These devices are called mechanical machines. Many modern machines, however, such as calculators and computers, have no moving parts. They are called electronic machines. Inside an electronic machine are lots of different components that are connected together to form circuits. These components control the way electricity flows around the circuits and so control what the machine does. Complicated electronic circuits, containing hundreds of thousands of components, can be contained on a single microchip a few millimetres across. Some electronic machines, such as weighing scales and digital watches, can replace the same mechanical machines. Many modern machines, such as robots, are combinations of mechanical and electronic parts.

An electronic calculator is a calculating machine. Inside is a microchip. Tiny electronic signals in the microchip's circuit do the calculations.

Weighing scale
When an orange is put on a scale, it presses on an electronic device called a strain gauge. The gauge controls the strength of a tiny electric current. Electronics inside the machine detect the size of the current, work out the orange's weight, and show it on a display.

Computers
A computer is a multi-purpose electronic machine. The job it does depends on the program it is using. A computer like this one can be used to play games, do complex calculations, paint pictures or communicate with other computers just by changing the program.

The first computers

This picture shows one of the first electronic computers. Called ENIAC (Electronic Numeral Integrator And Calculator), it was built in the 1940s. It took up a huge amount of space because its electronic parts were thousands of times bigger than today's microchips. ENIAC needed several rooms to fit in all its valves, wires and dials, but it was less powerful than a modern pocket calculator.

Inside a computer system

A computer is an extremely complicated machine, but the way it works is quite easy to understand if you think of it in several parts. Each part does its own job, such as storing or sending information.

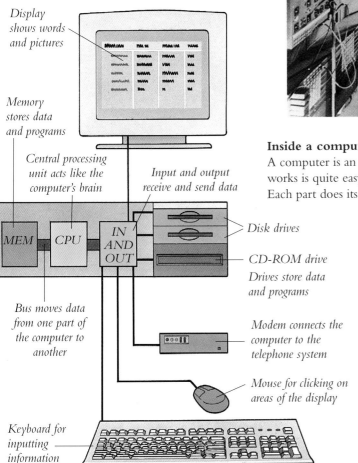

Display shows words and pictures

Memory stores data and programs

Central processing unit acts like the computer's brain

Input and output receive and send data

MEM CPU IN AND OUT

Disk drives

CD-ROM drive

Drives store data and programs

Bus moves data from one part of the computer to another

Modem connects the computer to the telephone system

Mouse for clicking on areas of the display

Keyboard for inputting information

FACT BOX

• In the 1830s, British scientist Charles Babbage designed a mechanical calculator called an Analytical Engine. Unfortunately, although it would have worked, it was never made because its parts were too complex.

• The first PC (personal computer) went on sale in 1975. It had 256 bytes of memory. An average PC today has 16 megabytes of memory – or more than 16 million bytes.

• The fastest supercomputers can add together more than a quarter of a million million numbers in a second.

MACHINES IN INDUSTRY

This steam-powered circular saw is cutting logs into shape. The saw has a razor-sharp blade with teeth that cut into the material as it spins. The object being cut is moved backwards or forwards across the blade.

MACHINE tools are machines that are used in factories to manufacture objects from metal, wood or other materials. The operations that machine tools carry out are cutting, drilling, grinding, turning and milling. Each of these operations is done by a special machine. For example, a lathe is used for turning and a saw is used for cutting. All machine tools have a cutting edge or blade, called a tool. The tool moves against the object being cut, called the workpiece. The tool shaves off unwanted material from the workpiece. Machine tools are used to make engine parts and other machines whose parts have to fit together perfectly. Industrial robots are versatile machines that can do many jobs, such as moving workpieces or drilling very accurately.

Turning
This pole lathe is powered by a foot operated pedal. The lathe spins the workpiece around very fast. The operator presses cutting tools against the spinning wood, shaving away a layer each time. How accurately the workpiece is finished depends on the skill of the operator.

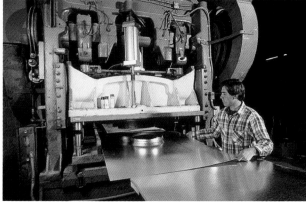
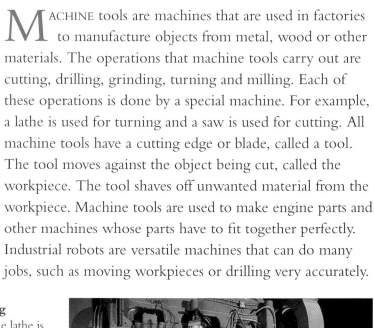

Pressing
This machine is called a die press. It presses flat sheets of steel into shaped panels, such as car bonnets. The top part of the machine moves down to do the pressing. Each sheet of steel is moulded to exactly the same shape every time.

Milling

This man is using a computer-controlled milling machine. The workpiece is spun in a lathe against a fixed cutting tool. In a milling machine, a toothed wheel cuts away the unwanted material. The computer controls the speed at which the lathe rotates and the position of the cutting tool. Computer-controlled machine tools make extremely accurate machine parts.

Cooling down

The milky liquid pouring on to this drill is coloured water. As the drill bit cuts into the metal workpiece, it gets very hot. The water keeps the drill cool, stopping the tool melting and washing waste metal away.

Industrial robots

These robots are welding car components together. The robot is shown how to do the job once and can then do it over and over again much faster than a human worker.

UNDER CONTROL

MACHINES that do complicated jobs need controls. Some of these machines need a human operator who controls the machine manually. For example, a car needs a driver to control its speed and direction. Other machines control themselves – once they are turned on, they do their job automatically. For example, an automatic washing machine washes and spins your clothes at the press of a button. One of the first machines to use a form of automatic control was the Jacquard loom. Punched paper cards were fed into the loom and told it which threads were to be used. Today, many machines are controlled by computer to perform a set task whenever it is required. The most advanced machines are even able to check their own work and change it if necessary.

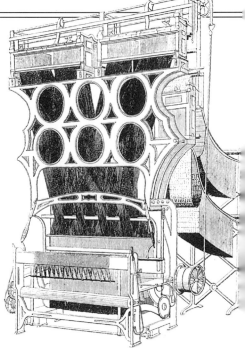

This Jacquard loom from 1851 was controlled by punch cards. The holes in the cards controlled the type of pattern the loom wove into the cloth. Changing the set of cards changed the pattern.

Like clockwork

Mechanical watches, like this one, have to control the speed at which their hands turn so that they keep the correct time. To do this, they have a device called a regulator. This makes sure the gears move at a regular speed.

Controlling speed

A steam locomotive's speed is controlled by a governor. If the speed increases, the metal balls spin out. This cuts down the amount of steam going to the engine, slowing it down.

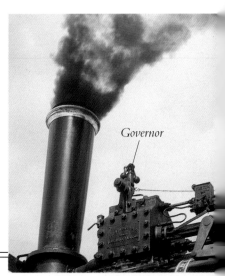

Governor

Industrial robots in car factories do many different jobs. These robots are delivering components to different areas of the factory. They are automatically guided by following lines on the floor. Under the lines are wires that make a magnetic field. The robots can detect this field and use it to follow a particular route around the factory. A central computer programmes the robots to pick up or deliver components around the factory.

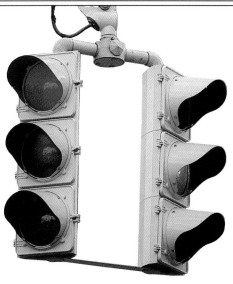

Controlling traffic

Traffic signals are controlled by electronics. Next time you are waiting at a set of traffic signals, try looking for the control box on the pavement. Some traffic lights are able to sense the arrival of vehicles and are programmed to regulate the flow of traffic. Other traffic lights operate on a timer.

FACT BOX

• In the 1700s and 1800s, watchmakers demonstrated their skills by building clockwork figures, called automata. The automata mimicked human actions, such as writing or playing musical instruments.

• Remote control is controlling a machine from a distance with long wires or using radio signals. Machines that work in dangerous situations, such as at great depths under the sea, are often remotely controlled.

Many of this car's systems are controlled by a microchip called a microprocessor. It continually checks signals from sensors and sends a control signal back again. It calculates the speed, distance and fuel consumption of the car and displays them on the dashboard.

AUTOMATIC CONTROL

Controlling a robot

1 Ask a friend to put on the blindfold. Use the list of commands opposite to direct your friend to where the egg is located.

ROBOTS are machines programmed to carry out actions in a similar way to humans. Robots seem very clever, but they can only do what they are told to do. The project below will show you how tricky it is to programme a robot to do even the simplest job. Using only words from the list of commands, see if you can get a friend to carry out the task successfully.

The second project shows you how to make a simple control disc. This is the sort of device used to control some washing machines. The metal track on the disc is part of an electric circuit. As the disc turns, the track completes or breaks the circuit, turning parts of the machine, such as lights and motors, on and off.

MATERIALS

You will need: blindfold, egg and egg-cup.

Robot commands
FORWARD
STOP
TURN LEFT
TURN RIGHT
ARM UP
ARM DOWN
CLOSE FINGERS
OPEN FINGERS

2 Your friend should not know where the egg is or what to do with it. Instruct your friend to carefully pick the egg up. Remember to only use commands in the list.

3 Now ask your friend to accurately place the egg on another surface. See if your friend can put it in the egg-cup. How quickly did your friend complete the task?

Make a control disc

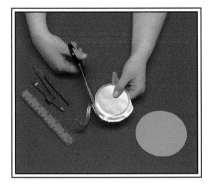

1 Using a compass, mark out a disc of card about 10 cm across and cut it out. Cut out the centre of the foil dish and glue it on to the card.

2 Put pieces of sticky tape across the foil track. The bare foil will complete the circuit. The pieces of sticky tape will break the circuit.

3 Using a paper fastener, mount the disc on to a piece of card. Using the wire, make two contacts with a bend in the middle, as shown.

MATERIALS

You will need: compass and pencil, ruler, card, scissors, aluminium foil dish, glue, sticky tape, paper fastener, wire, three plastic-coated wires, battery, torch bulb and holder.

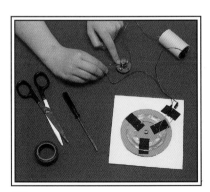

4 Stick the contacts to the card so that they press on the foil track. Make up a circuit with a battery, three wires and a bulb.

5 Attach two wires from the circuit to the two contacts. Turn the disc slowly. The light bulb should go on and off as the disc turns. As the contacts go over a piece of sticky tape, the circuit is broken and the light will go out. When they touch the foil again, the circuit is completed and the light will go back on. Do you know why the foil completes the electric circuit?

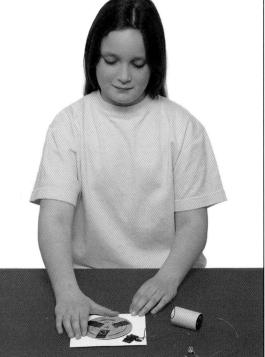

PERPETUAL MOTION

Every machine needs some sort of energy to make it work. The energy might come from a human or an animal, from a fuel, from electricity, or from the movement of wind or water. When the source of energy is taken away, the machine comes to a stop. Even if the machine is not doing any work, such as lifting or cutting, it will still come to a stop because of friction between its moving parts. Friction is the force that acts like a brake on the movement of most objects. It occurs as objects rub, or move, against each other. Before inventors understood the force of friction, they thought it would be possible to build perpetual motion machines – machines, which once they were started, would keep on going for ever.

You can feel friction at work by rubbing your hands together. The harder you press, the more difficult it is to move them. Can you feel the heat made by friction?

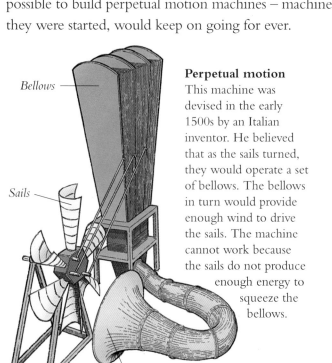

Bellows

Sails

Funnel

Perpetual motion
This machine was devised in the early 1500s by an Italian inventor. He believed that as the sails turned, they would operate a set of bellows. The bellows in turn would provide enough wind to drive the sails. The machine cannot work because the sails do not produce enough energy to squeeze the bellows.

Flywheels
A grinding wheel is used to sharpen tools. The wheel is very heavy and the grinding action does not slow it down much. A wheel like this is called a flywheel. It carries on spinning much longer than a light wheel would do.

Overcoming friction

Moving things by rolling, rather than sliding, cuts down friction. These rollerblades contain ball bearings around the wheel axles, where friction is at its greatest. They help the wheel move round smoothly, reducing friction and wear. Bearings are used in the moving parts of many small and large machines.

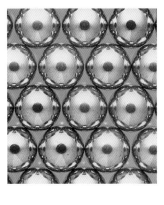

These ball bearings are suspended in oil. They are used to keep the moving parts of a machine separate so that they do not rub together and cause friction. This extends the life of the machine because it is the bearings and not the machine that wear out.

Frictionless Space

Things moving through air and water also encounter friction. As they move, the air and water resist the object and slow it down. There is no air in Space, so there is nothing to slow down a spacecraft once it has started moving. This might seem like perpetual motion, but it is not. Eventually, the spacecraft will crash into a star or a planet.

This racing car both uses and tries to overcome friction. Friction helps its tyres grip the road. Its smooth, streamlined shape, however, is designed to cut down drag, allowing it to travel faster. Drag is like friction – it tries to slow things that are moving through the air.

INDEX

PICTURE CREDITS

b=bottom, t=top, c=centre, l=left, r=right
Ancient Art and Architecture Collection Ltd: page 8. Ancient Egypt Picture Library: page 18t&b. Aviation Photographs International: page 37c. Barnaby's Picture Library/Gerald Clyde page 25bl. Bruce Coleman Ltd: pages 32bl&r, 33t; /Massimo Borchi page 15c; /Janos Jurka page 11; /Harald Lange page 5tr; /Neil McAllister page 62; /H P Merten page 57bl. Ecoscene: pages 32t, 49bl; /Gryniewicz page 56bl; /Nick Hawkes pages 19tr, 48bl; /W Lawler page 20bl; /M Maidment page 51b; /Sally Morgan page 16; /Towse page 52. E.T. Archive: pages 15t, 24, 46, 48t, 53, 55. Mary Evans Picture Library: page 29b. Holt Studios International: /Ivan Belcher pages 50bl, 58br; /Nigel Cattlin pages 48br, 50bl, 51c; /Paul McCullagh page 7; /Primrose Peacock page 56t; /Inga Spence page 51t. ICCE/Mark Boulton page 5bl. Image Bank: pages 15b, 19b. Planet Earth Pictures: pages 19tl; 63br. Quadrant: pages 25br, 37t, 47b; /Auto Express page 59b; /Anthony R Dalton page 47t; /Bryn Williams page 63bl. Science Museum/Science & Society Picture Library: page 43t&b. Science Photo Library: page 58t; /Dr Jeremy Burgess page 63tr; /Vaughan Fleming page 29c; /Food & Drug Administration page 56br; /Adam Hart-Davis page 25t; /Sheila Terry page 57t; /Rosenfeld Images Ltd pages 57br, 59tl; /David Parker page 58bl. Superstock: pages 5tl, 49br. Tony Stone: pages 39t, 47c. Trip: /Joynson-Hicks page 36t; /H Rogers pages 10, 49tr&l. Zefa: pages 5br, 20br, 33bl&r, 36b, 39b, 54, 59tr, 63tl; /Dieter Pittius page 26.